Physical Touch Love Language For Men

Unlocking The Secret Language Of Male Love And Affection

William R. Johnson

CONTENT

CHAPTER ONE

Understanding The Power Of Physical Touch

Physical touch is a vital part of human interaction and has the potential to express emotions and generate a strong feeling of connection between persons. It is a vital aspect of human connections, and it plays a critical role in the development of social, emotional, and cognitive abilities. In this chapter, we will discuss the significance of Physical touchin human interactions, how it affects the brain and body, and the cultural and socioeconomic variables that impact men's views towards physical touch.

The Significance Of Physical Touch In Human Relationships

Physical Touch is a strong technique for transmitting feelings and showing love, compassion, and concern. It is a natural means of connecting and developing a feeling of closeness between persons, and it plays a significant part in human interactions. Studies have revealed that physical touch has significant advantages for both physical and mental well-being. For example, it may decrease stress levels, reduce anxiety and depression, and increase general well-being. Physical touch has also been demonstrated to promote immunological function, lessen pain perception, and increase emotions of social support and connection.

Additionally, Physical touch is vital in the development of social, emotional, and cognitive abilities, particularly in early life. Infants need Physical touch to acquire a feeling of trust, safety, and security, and it is vital for their healthy emotional and social development. Physical touch helps to regulate a baby's body temperature, heart rate, and respiration, and it generates a feeling of security and safety.

As children grow older, Physical touch continues to play a critical role in their emotional and social development, allowing them to create healthy attachments and interactions with others.

How Physical Touch Affects The Brain And Body

Physical touch may have a significant impact on a variety of physiological and psychological processes, as well as the brain and body. For instance, Physical touch may cause the release of oxytocin, a hormone that is essential for attachment, trust, and other socially important behaviors. Physical contact, such as embracing, holding hands, or kissing, releases oxytocin, which fosters emotions of coziness, love, and connection. Moreover, it aids in lowering blood pressure, reducing stress levels, and encouraging feelings of peace and relaxation.

Physical touch has also been shown to stimulate the somatosensory cortex, insula, and amygdala, among other brain regions. The insula is engaged in emotional processing and awareness, while the somatosensory cortex is in charge of processing sensory data such as touch. An important part of controlling emotions, notably fear, and anxiety, is played by the amygdala. Certain parts of the brain may become active by physical contact, which triggers the release of neurotransmitters like dopamine and serotonin, which are essential for controlling mood and emotion.

Elements From Culture And Society That Affect Men's Attitudes About Touch

Men are often trained to avoid or reduce Physical touchas a means of expressing emotions, despite the many advantages of physical touch. This is due to social and cultural variables that affect how males see physical contact. Physical touch is often connected to a lack of strength, fragility, or femininity in many cultures where males are supposed to be emotionally aloof, independent, and powerful individuals. Men may find it difficult as a result to physically connect with people and convey their feelings.

Men are often prevented from making Physical touch with other males since this is seen to go against socially accepted standards of masculinity and sexuality. Men's Physical touch is often stigmatized and connected to homosexuality or other types of misbehavior. Men may feel alone and disconnected as a result of this, which makes it difficult for them to develop fulfilling ties and relationships.

Understanding Your Love Language Through Touch

While Physical touch is a common method to show love, how we choose to express and receive it varies from person to person. We'll look at the five love languages and how they relate to Physical touch in this chapter. We will also go through how to choose your preferred kind of Physical touch and how to express it to your partner.

The Five Love Languages And Physical Touch Concerning Them

The five love languages identified by Dr. Gary Chapman include words of affirmation, spending time with others, getting gifts, doing acts of service, and physical contact. Each individual has a preferred method of receiving love, adoration, and care, known as their main love language. Knowing your partner's love language may help you build a stronger connection with them and enhance your relationship.

One of the five love languages is physical contact, which entails utilizing touch to convey feelings of love and affection. Yet, based on a person's preferences, Physical touch may be presented and received in a variety of ways. For instance, some individuals choose to give hugs to communicate their affection, while others favor holding hands or giving massages. Similar to how some individuals choose to express their affection by hugging or kissing, some others prefer softer kinds of contact like a pat on the back or a light touch on the arm.

What Is My Main Physical Touch Language Of Love?

Knowing your preferred Physical touchTo strengthen your connection with your lover, learn their love language. To choose your preferred method of communication, consider the following:

1. How do I like to contact people physically?
2. How do I like to be touched physically by others?
3. What kinds of Physical touch elicit the most feelings of love and caring in me?

4. What kind of Physical touch makes me feel better when I'm unhappy or under pressure?

You may determine which of these is your preferred Physical touch love language based on your responses to these questions. For instance, if you like to provide and receive Physical touching in the form of hugs, cuddles, and holding hands, then physical touch may be your preferred form of communication.

How To Tell Your Spouse Your Love Language

It's crucial to let your spouse know what your preferred kind of Physical touch is after you've determined this. In every relationship, communication is essential, and expressing your wants and preferences may help you get to know your spouse better.

Use the following advice to let your partner know your partner's love language for physical touch:

1. Describe your love language to your spouse. Describe how Physical touch makes you feel cherished and cared for.

2. Give your spouse concrete examples of the kinds of Physical touch you enjoy, such as holding hands, embracing, or snuggling.

3. Demonstrate how to physically contact your spouse: If your partner is unclear about how to physically touch you, demonstrate for them in a manner that feels comfortable to you.

4. Find out your partner's love language. By knowing your partner's love language,

you can build a stronger connection with them and have a better relationship overall.

5. Be open to compromise: It's important to be open to compromise and find a method to satisfy each other's demands since your spouse may have a different Physical touch love language than you do.

Understanding your partner's love language for Physical touch is a crucial first step in enhancing your connection. You may better convey your wants and preferences to your spouse by being aware of how you like to express and receive physical contact. This will also help you build a stronger connection. You may create a better and more rewarding relationship with your spouse by letting them know how much you value physical contact.

CHAPTER TWO

Getting Beyond Physical Touch Barriers

While Physical touch is a potent means of expressing love and compassion, it may be challenging for some men to provide or accept physical touch. In this chapter, we'll look at some typical obstacles males have when expressing their desire for Physical touch and provide solutions. We will also go through how to create a space that is secure and welcoming for physical contact.

Several Obstacles Guys Face While Offering Physical Touch

At an early age, men are often trained to repress their feelings and refrain from showing weakness. As a consequence, when it comes to physical contact, many men may feel awkward or humiliated. Some typical obstacles that stop males from expressing Physical touch are as follows:

1. Fear of rejection: Men may worry that their spouse will reject them or that their Physical touch won't be returned.

2. Fear of exposure: Men may feel exposed or vulnerable while expressing Physical touch since it calls for a certain amount of emotional openness and vulnerability.

3. Societal conditioning: The expectation that males should be tough and emotionally indifferent is often reinforced by society, which causes men to repress their emotions and shun physical contact.

4. Prior trauma: Men who have gone through mental or physical trauma may find it hard to express Physical touch since it might bring up painful memories.

How To Get Rid Of Your Shame, Insecurity, And Fear Of Physical Touch

Physical touch-related fear, guilt, and insecurities must be overcome, and this calls for a desire to be open to change and be vulnerable. Men may use the following techniques to get beyond these obstacles:

1. Disprove limiting ideas: Men may have limiting views about physical contact, such as that it indicates weakness or is unmanly. Men may learn to feel more at ease with Physical touch by challenging these ideas and replacing them with empowering ones.

2. Engage in mindfulness exercises: Activities like meditation and deep breathing that promote awareness may assist men in being more attentive to their thoughts and feelings. Men who have more self-awareness may be able to recognize and overcome their Physical touch limitations.

3. Speak with a dependable partner: Men may feel more supported and validated when they talk to a dependable companion about their anxieties and phobias around physical contact. Also, it may assist males in creating techniques

for expressing Physical touch in a manner that is secure and at ease.

4. Get professional assistance: Men who have undergone trauma or who have significant emotional problems may benefit from professional assistance, such as therapy or counseling.

Techniques For Establishing A Comfortable And Secure Environment For Physical Touch

Men may feel more at ease expressing Physical touching a secure and comfortable setting is provided. Here are some ideas for creating a welcoming and secure environment:

1. Establish clear limits: Men may feel more at ease and in control when there are boundaries surrounding physical contact. Men may feel safer if limits are established about the kind of touch or the duration of physical contact, for instance.

2. Start small: Men may progressively grow more comfortable with Physical touch by beginning with tiny, non-threatening physical touches, such as a pat on the back or a handshake.

3. Employ positive affirmations: Men may overcome unfavorable thoughts about Physical touch and increase their self-confidence by repeating affirmations like "I am deserving of love and compassion."

4. Exercise consent: When it comes to physical contact, permission is essential. Men should always inquire about and respect their partner's Physical touch preferences and limits.

It might be difficult to go over physical discomfort, but it's necessary to forge long-lasting, wholesome connections. Men may become more at ease and confident in expressing Physical touch by acknowledging and overcoming their worries, and insecurities, and limiting ideas about it.

CHAPTER THREE

Aesthetics Of Touch

Physical touch may transmit a broad variety of feelings, from love and affection to desire and passion, making it a very effective instrument for communication.

The many forms of touch and what they mean:

1. The purpose of affectionate contact is to elicit feelings of love, warmth, and compassion. Hugs, kissing, and snuggling are all part of it.

2. Supporting Touch: This kind of touching aims to reassure and soothe the recipient. It involves holding hands, giving someone a pat on the back, and putting your hand on their shoulder.

3. This kind of contact is intended to be lighthearted and enjoyable. It involves wrestling, tickling, and amusing slaps.

4. Sexual Touch: This kind of contact is used to show closeness and desire. Kissing, cuddling, and sexual touch are all included.

How To Express Love, Compassion, And Desire With Touch:

1. Be Aware of Your Partner's Love Language: Keep in mind that different individuals have various forms of love, and not everyone may respond well to physical contact. Make sure you are using touch in a manner that speaks to your spouse following their preferred language of love.

2. Pay Attention to Body Language: Be aware of your partner's nonverbal cues and react appropriately. It may indicate that they are not in the mood or that

something is upsetting them if they seem uneasy or resistant to touch.

3. Start Small and Build Up: If you're uncertain about your partner's tolerance for contact, start small and increase the amount of time you spend together over time. This might facilitate the creation of a secure and inviting environment for touch.

4. Employ Touch to Show Your Love and Appreciation: Touching your spouse may be a potent method to show your love and appreciation for them. To express your love and devotion, a simple hug or kiss may be quite effective.

How To Perfect The Art Of Touch

1. Develop a mindfulness practice: Being aware of your own body and senses might make it easier for you to understand your partner's wants and needs.

2. Be Honest and Transparent in Your Communication: When it comes to touch, communication is essential. Be upfront and truthful with your spouse about your own goals and limitations, and be open to their suggestions.

3. Experiment with Various Touches: Don't be scared to try out various touches

to see which ones you and your partner respond to the best.

4. Embrace Consent and Respect: Always remember that touching should be courteous and voluntary. Be sure to respect your partner's limits and to often check in with them.

It takes time and effort to perfect the art of touch, but it can be a very pleasant and rewarding method to express your love and affection to your spouse. Understanding the many sorts of touch, using it to express your love, affection, and desire, and implementing our advice for perfecting the art of touch can help you build a stronger, more meaningful relationship with your partner.

Increasing Intimacy With Touch

Building closeness in a relationship requires physical touch regularly. It can strengthen bonds, foster stronger emotional ties, and advance general well-being.

How Touching Each Other Can Increase Intimacy in a Relationship:

1. Physical touch fosters a sense of safety and security: Trust and intimacy can only

be developed when couples feel safe and secure with one another.

2. Physical touch encourages connection and communication: Touch may aid couples in establishing nonverbal connections and communication, which can result in deeper emotional bonds.

3. Physical touch may improve one's physical and mental health by releasing chemicals such as dopamine and oxytocin that are good for both.

How To Utilize Touch To Strengthen Your Partner's Emotional Connection

1. Emphasize quality over quantity: What matters is the quality of the touch, not the number of it. Instead of simply going through the motions, put your attention on establishing purposeful, meaningful touch.

2. Be present and attentive: While exchanging physical contact, be careful to do so. Throw all outside noise aside and concentrate just on your lover and the touch.

3. Employ touch as a means of communication: Touch may be a potent means of expressing emotions, wants, and desires.

4. Try various forms of touch to see which ones are most effective for you and your partner. This can involve holding hands, kissing, massaging, and having sexual contact.

Practical Activities To Improve Physical Touch Intimacy:

1. The Holding of Hands Hold hands while facing your partner while seated. Use

your hands to explore various touch sensations and motions by taking turns leading and following.

2. The Hugging Exercise: Swap embraces and experiment with various hug styles, such as a tight embrace or a gradual, soothing hug.

3. The Massage Exercise: Alternate providing and receiving a full-body massage, paying special attention to establishing a calming and private atmosphere.

4. The Sensory Exercise: With your partner blindfolded, utilize various tactile

stimuli to pique their senses, such as feathers, ice cubes, or lotion.

Physical touch has the potential to significantly increase intimacy in a relationship. Couples may strengthen their emotional bond and advance general welfare by emphasizing quality over quantity, being present and attentive, utilizing touch as a means of communication, and experimenting with various sorts of contact.

Physical Touch Expression In Many Contexts

For many males, expressing Physical touch in various contexts may be difficult. Using physical touch to communicate in both public and private settings:

1. Public Settings: When expressing physical touch in public, more discretion is required. A short kiss on the cheek, a gentle touch on the arm or back, or holding hands are all acceptable kinds of Physical touch in public.

2. Private Settings: There are more opportunities to express physical touch in

private settings. All types of physical contact, including cuddling, hugging, kissing, and sexual contact, is acceptable in private.

Techniques For Getting Around Physical Touch's Various Cultural And Social Norms:

1. Recognize your community's cultural and social norms around physical contact: As various cultures have varied cultural and social norms regarding physical contact, it's critical to know what is and is not appropriate.

2. Respect limits: Regardless of your cultural or social background, it's crucial to respect others' boundaries and be sensitive to their needs.

3. Express your needs: If you need certain forms of Physical touch from your spouse, be sure to respectfully and lovingly let them know.

How To Respectfully And Lovingly Express Your Needs For Physical Touch

1. Be precise and explicit: When expressing your desire for physical

contact, be precise and clear about what you need and why.

2. Employ "I" statements: To avoid appearing accusing or blaming, use "I" phrases when articulating your requirements for physical contact.

3. Listen to your spouse: Expressing your needs to your partner is just as vital as listening to theirs. Be willing to make concessions and find a resolution that benefits you both.

Understanding cultural and societal conventions, upholding boundaries, and respectfully and lovingly expressing your desire for Physical touch make it simpler to express yourself physically in a variety of circumstances. Couples may handle Physical touch in a manner that fosters closeness, respect, and love by being explicit and detailed, utilizing "I" words, and listening to their spouse.

Getting Beyond Physical Touch Obstacles

Although showing love and care via Physical touch may be a potent and rewarding experience, it can also be difficult for many men.

Partnerships involving physical touch often face these difficulties:

One of the most frequent problems in relationships involving physical touch is when one spouse wants more Physical touch than the other.

2. Busy schedules: It might be difficult to find time for Physical touch due to work, family, and social responsibilities.

3. Stress: For males who may find it difficult to convey vulnerability, stress, and worry can make Physical touch challenging.

How To Solve Problems With Regularity, Initiation, And Reciprocity

1. Communicate: In every relationship, communication is essential, but it's crucial when it comes to physical contact. Be open and sincere with your spouse about your wants and needs, and pay attention to theirs as well.

2. Be ready to compromise: It may be challenging to find a middle ground when it comes to the frequency, initiation, and reciprocity of physical contact.

3. Use your imagination; Physical touch isn't only for the bedroom. Discover methods to include physically touching your daily interactions, such as holding hands when you walk, snuggling on the sofa while you watch TV, or massaging one another.

Top Tips For Sustaining A Relationship With Healthy And Satisfying Physical Touch:

1. Set aside time for physical contact: Despite your hectic schedules, it's crucial to arrange a time for physical contact. Plan frequent date evenings or allot a

certain period each day for snuggling or other types of physical contact.

2. Pay attention to your partner's nonverbal clues and adjust your behavior appropriately. Provide a hug or a soothing touch if they feel nervous or anxious.

3. Mindfulness training may assist you in being focused and in the now when receiving physical contact. Be present and pay attention to your feelings as much as you can.

Conclusion

Physical touch relationships may be difficult, but by talking things out, making concessions, and using their imaginations, couples can get over problems with frequency, initiation, and reciprocity. Maintaining a satisfying and healthy physical touch connection may also be facilitated by scheduling regular physical contact, paying attention, and engaging in mindfulness exercises. Couples may establish a strong and enduring relationship by emphasizing Physical touch and being open and honest with one another.

www.ingramcontent.com/pod-product-compliance
Lightning Source LLC
Chambersburg PA
CBHW050749250726
48662CB00005B/2104